10 Natural Ways to Support a Healthy Immune System Without Vaccines

Table of Contents

About The Author iv

Introduction 1

I. The Diet That Supports A Healthy Immune System 3

II. Supplements 11

III. How Chiropractic Saved Lives During
The 1918 Flu Pandemic 24

IV. Sleep 30

V. Exercise 32

VI. Sauna.. 34

VII. Recipes 37

VIII. Essential oils and Colloidal Silver 46

IX. Pandemic humor 52

X. The Real Pandemic Is Insulin Resistance 56

Addendum.. 61

Recommended YouTube Videos 64

Conclusion 65

References.. 67

About the Author

Dr. Raphael Rettner is a Palmer College of Chiropractic West graduate and has been in practice since 1982. Dr. Rettner is one of the most highly skilled and respected chiropractors in the United States. He has made numerous radio and T.V. appearances, is the author of *Vegetarian Cooking for People with Allergies* and has produced several DVDs including: *End P.M.S Now!, The Ultimate Diet,* and *Twelve Causes of an Unstable Spine.* He has studied both force and non-force techniques such as Advanced Biostructural Correction, Applied Kinesiology, Biophysics, Gonstead, S.O.T. and over a dozen others. With a combination of creative thinking and an insatiable quest for knowledge, Dr. Rettner has developed several new and exciting chiropractic techniques. Since 1994 he has taught these in his Applied Trigger Points seminar to chiropractors all across the United States, Australia, Canada and England.

You can reach Raphael by e-mail drrettner@sbcglobal.net or by phone at 925-962-9160

Introduction

I hope you're doing well amidst this Covid 19 flu crisis. Over the past few months I have spent several hours consulting with a well known nutritionist and a functional medicine doctor who offer their sage advice about how to support a healthy immune system. I have edited this information down to a more practical and user-friendly version. I have included tips on which diet, supplements, herbs and essential oils are best to help the immune system and where to get them. In the future, I also have included information about how chiropractic, sleep, exercise and saunas support a healthy immune system. As a special bonus, I've included easy to make recipes to assist you in keeping your immune system healthy. The first 2 chapters includes a list of common supplements recommended in order to support a healthy immune system and which foods are high in each nutrient. Your immune system is your defense to fight off and protect you against pathogens that cause disease. Be sure to mark the foods you like to eat in each category but are not currently eating and start to include them in your diet.

"We're all waiting for a vaccine, and if they come up with a vaccine and they've actually done real safety testing on it, and the vaccine works, I would be happy to have the vaccine. But the problem is they're not [safety] testing it at this point."-Robert F Kennedy Jr. If you choose to take a vaccine, make sure it's safety tested with double blind controls. Mercury, aluminum and formaldehyde are known additives to the vaccines. It's also a non-liability product, thus the drug companies can't get sued if you have an adverse reaction.

Medical experts are not giving us the whole picture. According to Dr. Hakim Djaballah, virologist and ex ceo of Pasteur Institute Korea, for the past 20 years many companies and researchers have promised us a vaccine for SARS-1. They tried and found this virus is not amenable to a vaccine. Because of that they may need several more years of research, but don't hold your breath. A vaccine helps with prevention by pointing to the immune system where to go. According to Dr. Mark Hyman M.D. "People who are immune compromised aren't helped by vaccines." According to Dietrich Klinghardt M.D., "Vaccines record is fairly poor. They're available on the market once the illness is almost gone. By that time the virus may mutate and it will no longer be effective."

Your immune system is what's going to help you. You can wait for a year or more for a vaccine to be developed or try to make your immune system stronger now.

If you'd like to be proactive and strengthen your immune system naturally, I'll be available for a complimentary 15 minute nutritional consultation to assist you in making the best diet and supplement choices for your individual needs. If you're not a current patient and would like to set up an appointment for a complimentary 15-minute nutritional consultation, or a chiropractic adjustment, you can contact me by phone at 925-962-9160 or e-mail drrettner@sbcglobal.net.

FREE 15 MINUTE NUTRITIONAL CONSULTATION
go to drrettner.com and scroll down to the bottom of the page.

I. The diet that supports a healthy Immune system

How to Support Your Immune System: Remember, Let Food Be Your Medicine! Good nutrition is essential, and vitamins C, and D and minerals such as zinc are good place to start, so says Harvard's School of Public Health;

— medicinal mushrooms can potentially augment various immune and pulmonary functions, so says the **National Cancer Institute**.

- **Cut out sugar and refined starches.** Now has never been a better time for a sugar and junk food detox. Studies have shown that refined sugars can suppress your immune system for hours after ingesting. Limiting starch and sugar will help your immune system function better and your overall health improves.

- After old age, obesity appears to be the most prominent risk factor for being hospitalized with COVID-19, doubling the risk of hospitalization in patients under the age of 60. Obesity also makes you more vulnerable to infectious diseases by causing chronic inflammation, which in turn, lowers your immune function. The real pandemic appears to be insulin resistance, a diet-induced condition. Higher blood glucose levels appear to play a significant role in viral replication. The inflammatory response to influenza infections is also known to drive up glucose metabolism. The virus needs the sugar to replicate.

- **Eat a whole foods, nutrient-dense diet**. Our immune system relies on nutrient-dense whole foods to function well.

- **Ensure adequate protein intake.** While most Americans eat adequate amounts of protein, some do not, such as the elderly and vegan populations. Protein is critical for immune function and protein malnutrition is a big risk factor for death from infections. Eat approximately 1 gram/kg or about half your body weight in grams of protein a day, or about two four-ounce servings of organic, clean animal protein. Plant-based proteins (legumes, nuts/seeds) are adequate if consumed in enough quantity. Try tempeh from non-GMO soy for the highest protein concentrations.

- **Add garlic, onions, ginger, and lots of spices (oregano, turmeric, rosemary) to your meals!** Add these to your soups and vegetable dishes, as well as bean dips and sauces. Garlic and onions offer wide spectrum antimicrobial properties.

- **Eat multiple servings of colorful fruits and vegetables** high in vitamins A and C, and phytonutrients that support the immune system. Choose more leafy greens, cruciferous vegetables (broccoli, Brussels sprouts, and cauliflower), peppers, sweet potatoes, and squashes. Aim for 2 servings of fruits and 8 or more servings of vegetables! A serving is half a cup.

- **Eat fermented foods to support your microbiome and immunity.** Eat sauerkraut, kimchi, natto, miso, tempeh, unsweetened yogurt, kefir.
- **Alkalize your body.** Sugar and processed foods tend to make your body slightly more acidic and more receptive to the COVID-19 virus. Eating whole plant foods and lots of them, 5 to 8 cups a day, is a good way to alkalinize your body. Try making big vegetable and bone broth soups which can help improve your pH.

- **Drink plenty of fluids, especially warmer fluids.** Consuming adequate fluids supports all your bodies' functions including the immune system. Make soups and broths from scratch with fresh vegetables and have them throughout the week. (See the recipe section in chapter VII.) Drink herbal teas like ginger and turmeric tea. Keep a bottle of filtered water with you at all times. Avoid concentrated fruit juices and sweetened beverages, as the sugar content is harmful for the immune system.

- **The ketogenic diet plus intermittent fasting** supports a healthy immune system. It can also be helpful for insulin resistance. Avoid the ketogenic diet if you have thyroid issues and if your gallbladder has been removed. If you have hypoglycemia (low blood sugar) avoid intermittent fasting.

Foods high in nutrients that help prevent colds and flus:

1. **Vitamin C** has the power to stimulate the production of white blood cells which are infection fighting cells. Start the day of the glass of lemon water. Vitamin C.

20 of the best foods that are high in vitamin C
1. Oranges
2. Acerola Cherries
3. Rose Hips
4. Chili Peppers
5. Guavas
6. Sweet Yellow & Red Bell Peppers
7. Blackcurrants
8. Thyme
9. Parsley
10. Mustard Spinach
11. Kale

12. Kiwis
13. Broccoli
14. Brussels Sprouts
15. Lemons
16. Lychees
17. Persimmons
18. Papayas
19. Strawberries
20. Plums

2. Vitamin D supports the T cells which are made by the thymus gland. can be found in. -

Vitamin D Rich Foods:
1. Wild caught salmon, grass fed butter and Mushrooms.
2. Wild Herring, wild Sardines and anchovies.
Next to sunlight, *cod liver oil* has the most concentrated natural source of this disease-preventing vitamin. Just one tablespoon of cod liver oil contains nearly 1,400 IU of vitamin D3.

3. Fish Oil-Sardines, halibut and salmon are an excellent source of Omega 3 fatty acids.
4. Zinc is the most important trace mineral for the immune system to keep it strong. It's very protective against viruses. Zinc can increase T cells.

Zinc-Rich Foods:
1. Meat-Lamb and Beef
2. Legumes-Hummus, baked beans, black beans and lentils.
3. Seeds-chia seeds, hemp seeds, pumpkin seeds
4. Nuts-walnuts It's found in mushrooms, spinach and red meat.

5. Probiotics-kimchi, miso and sauerkraut

6. Garlic kills off bacteria, virus, yeast and mold. Garlic's immune-boosting properties seem to come from a heavy concentration of the sulfur-containing compound allicin.

7. **Coconut oil**-the coronavirus is a lipid coded virus that doesn't do well in the presence of medium chain triglyceride. Coconut oil is our best source of these healthy fats.

8. **Bone Broth**- Bone broth is made by simmering the bones and connective tissue of animals. This highly nutritious stock is commonly used in soups, sauces and gravies. It has also recently gained popularity as a health drink. Animal bones are rich in calcium, magnesium, potassium, phosphorus and other trace minerals — the same minerals needed to build and strengthen your own bones.

Connective tissue gives you glucosamine and chondroitin, natural compounds found in cartilage that are known to support joint health.

Marrow provides vitamin A, vitamin K2, minerals like zinc, iron, boron, manganese and selenium, as well as omega-3 and omega-6 fatty acids. **Bone broth** has been shown to help seal openings in the gut that may lead to an overactive and eventually weakened **immune system**. **Bone broth** is easy for the body to absorb, can help heal and seal the gut, and also has anti-inflammatory properties.

9. **Anti-viral herbs**: Many herbs have broad-spectrum antimicrobial effects or immune-enhancing effects. Immune boosters include astragalus, echinacea, green tea extract and andrographis.

Ten best natural antibiotic foods:

1. Garlic. Cultures across the world have long recognized garlic for its preventive and curative powers. ...

2. Honey. Since the time of Aristotle, honey has been used as an ointment that helps wounds to heal and prevents or draws out infection. ...

3. Ginger is another ingredient many turn to after getting sick. Ginger may help decrease inflammation, which can help reduce a sore throat and other inflammatory illnesses. Ginger may also help decrease nausea. While it's used in many sweet desserts, ginger packs   some heat in the form of gingerol, a relative of capsaicin. Ginger may help decrease chronic pain.

4. Echinacea

5. Goldenseal

6. Clove

7. Oregano

8. Turmeric is anti-inflammatory.

10. Green tea is packed with flavonoids, a type of antioxidant. Green tea is also a good source of the amino acid L-theanine may aid in the production of germ-fighting compounds in your T-cells.

Eight of the top mushrooms with immune-supportive properties:

Mushroom Extracts such as Chaga, Lion's Mane reishi, maitake, Oyster, shiitake, turkey tail, and cordyceps provide immune-supporting properties. For centuries, people around the world have turned to mushrooms for a healthy immune system...

"Studies show that mushrooms increase the production and activity of white blood cells, making them more aggressive.

Shiitake is an excellent choice of **mushroom** to **boost immune system** due to its high B vitamins, vitamin D, selenium, niacin, **and** 7 of **the** 8 essential amino acids. ... Shiitake has shown robust anti-cancer activity, primarily through enhancing immune function. Cooking with medicinal mushrooms like shiitake is also helpful.

Mushrooms particularly **shiitake, maitake, reishi, shimeji** and **oyster** varieties – are good sources of beta-glucans. The beta-glucans in mushrooms have been shown to boost the innate immune system function, which is the first line of defense against viruses and bacteria. It helps your white blood cells bind to and kill viruses and bacteria. The Beta-glucans in mushrooms helps reduce the severity of influenza infection and lowers influenza mortality in animal studies. Cooking with medicinal mushrooms like shiitake is also helpful. Reishi mushrooms can be helpful to take in the evening to calm the body to prepare for sleep.

II. Supplements to Support a Healthy Immune System

During the coronavirus frenzy there have been an increasing number of health claims and the promotion of many different supplements. It's easy to become overwhelmed with all the choices. After consulting with a well known nutritionist and a functional medicine doctor, I've narrowed down all the choices to a sensible few.

Let's start with an overview of the vitamins, minerals and herbs you need for Basic Immune Support and why they are important.

Basic Immune Support:

- **Multivitamin/Mineral:** This is the foundation for any health support regimen. It's a good way to cover the basic vitamins and minerals your body needs for day-to-day functions. If you aren't on a good multivitamin it's a good idea to get and stay on one. Look for a high-quality, broad-spectrum multivitamin and mineral. I recommend All in One from Holistic Health.

- **ALL IN ONE™ MULTI-VITAMIN / MINERAL**   All in One- has the nutrients needed to support a healthy methylation cycle as well as basic nutritional needs. It took over a decade to finalize this multivitamin/mineral formula.

- **Buffered Vitamin C:** The role of vitamin C in supporting the immune system has long been known. Take 500-1,000mg throughout the day with meals and snacks. I recommend Ecological Formulas Buffered Vitamin C Crystals 1 teaspoon contains:

2500mg Vitamin C (Made from tapioca, so it's easy on the digestive tract.)

Buffered Vitamin C Crystals from Ecological Formulas is a dietary supplement designed to assist in neutralizing hyperacidity associated with ascorbic acid.

These Vitamin C crystals are derived from a non-corn source and contain absolutely no corn antigens.

he nutrients in this formula are the purest and highest quality available and contain no preservatives, diluents, sweetening agents or chemical additives.

The minerals occur in a bicarbonate form which has a buffering action and makes a sparkling, effervescent drink.*

* This statement has not been evaluated by the Food and Drug Administration. This product is not intended to diagnose, treat, cure, or prevent any disease.

- **Vitamin D3:** Get Extra Lung Immunity With This Vitamin. To give your lungs an immunity jumpstart, I recommend boosting your vitamin D3 levels.

  Vitamin D3 keeps your immune system running smoothly and helps it ward off infections, including colds, and flu — especially when they impact the lungs and respiratory health. Studies show that your airways, alveoli and bronchial tubes are **packed with vitamin D3 receptors**, whose actions produce and support a range of immune fighter cells in your lungs — including antimicrobial peptides, alveolar macrophages, as well as T and B cells.

  Here are ways to boost your vitamin D3 levels:

  Take a D3 supplement. Make sure the vitamin D supplement you take is vitamin D3. It's the same vitamin D3 your body produces. Just be sure to avoid the synthetic form of vitamin D2 that's found in most multivitamins, because it is less potent and less absorbable. Having your D3 levels checked by your doctor is the best way to know for sure. Vitamin D may help with normal immune function and can contribute to a balanced mood. Adequate vitamin D status is critical for optimal immune function and this cannot be achieved without supplementation during the winter months. Studies have shown that people with vitamin D deficiency are 11 times more likely to get a cold or flu. Supplementing with vitamin D has been found to reduce colds and flu by 42%.

It is best to get your levels of 25-OH vitamin D checked for accurate dosing. Blood levels should be above 30 ng/dl, however, optimal levels are probably closer to 50ng/dl for most. Many need 5,000 IU or more of vitamin D3 a day in the winter.

Special Note: The Sun and Vitamin D. With 30 minutes of daily sun exposure (without sunscreen) during the summer months, your body is capable of producing 50,000 IU of vitamin D3 over the following 24 hours. Get out and catch some rays at least a few times per week — if not every day.

Regular **sun** exposure is the most natural way to get enough **vitamin D**. It protects against pathogens and kills microbes. To maintain healthy blood levels, aim to get 10–30 minutes of midday sunlight, several times per week. People with darker skin may need a little more than this. I recommend starting with *at least* 2,000 IUs a day for adults from a good supplement — preferably in the morning. 1,000 IU for children. That leaves plenty of room for you to get additional vitamin D from other sources. Doses of 5,000 IU to 8,000 IU may be needed depending on your individual needs. Vitamin D is very effective when taken in conjunction with vitamin K. Therefore I recommend Vitamin D3K2 from Quicksilver Scientific. I also recommend Liqua D from Apex Energetics.*

*This statement has not been evaluated by the Food and Drug Administration. This product is not intended to diagnose, treat, cure, or prevent any disease.

- **Nanoemulsified Cat's Claw Elite®**

Cat's Claw Elite is an immune supportive formula, which is enhanced with lemon balm plant-derived essential oil, Vitamin D and the fatty acid monolaurin, all designed to maximally protect the immune system.

DESCRIPTION

Store this product at Room Temperature.

Each 1 mL of Nanoemulsified Cat's Claw Elite® delivers 1000 IU of Vitamin D3 and 350 mg of a proprietary blend of Liquid Cat's Claw bark extract, phospholipids (from purified sunflower seed lecithin), monolaurin, Liquid Lemon Balm leaf extract, Lemon Balm leaf oil, Rose flower oil, Natural Mint oil.

Cat's Claw is a climbing vine that thrives in the Peruvian rainforest—stretching as tall as a thousand feet. Medicinal use of the inner bark dates back 2,000 years to the Inca civilization, and to this day South American Ashaninka priests regard the plant as sacred, using it for healing and in religious ceremonies.

The most widely utilized strain of cat's claw, Uncaria tomentosa, boasts a treasure trove of phytonutrients thought to be responsible for the vine's reputed healing powers and ability to strengthen immune defenses.

The fatty acid monolaurin is derived from lauric acid, and is formed naturally in the human body in small quantities. Monolaurin works by binding directly to the lipid-protein envelope of invaders, preventing them from attaching and entering cells. Vitamin D is added to aid normal immune system function and bone health.

Because many herbs have low bioavailability when taken orally, I recommend from Nanoemulsified Cat's Claw Elite®

from Quicksilver Scientific. Dr. Shade developed. Liposomal delivery systems that have been shown to lead to more immediate effects. In addition to exceptional absorption rates, small liposomal and nanoemulsified particles bypass digestive enzymes and breakdown in the liver. The liposomes in this formula contain pure phosphatidylcholine, a lipid that is the primary building block of all cell membranes.*

*This statement has not been evaluated by the Food and Drug Administration. This product is not intended to diagnose, treat, cure, or prevent any disease.

- **Zinc: Zinc** is essential for the maintenance of immune system strength and glandular health. Zinc promotes immune system health by activating the production of white blood cells. It can be rapidly depleted when the body is fighting an illness. If you have a bout of the flu or a viral infection, your body uses zinc in huge quantities to maintain your immune system. Two of the symptoms of COVID-19 are loss of the sense of smell and taste. They are also 2 signs of a zinc deficiency. You can take an additional supplement or consume more foods high in this powerful immune-supporting nutrient. Seafood— especially oysters—red meat, and pumpkin seeds are the best food sources. I recommend taking 30 drops per day of

Eidon's ionic liquid zinc. It's more easily absorbed than zinc tablets and is usually available.*

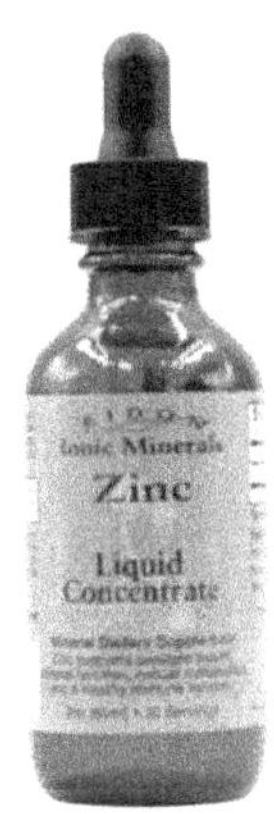

* This statement has not been evaluated by the Food and Drug Administration. This product is not intended to diagnose, treat, cure, or prevent any disease.

- **Probiotics:** A healthy gut flora supports a healthy gut, a major barrier against pathogens and integral to the immune system.
  I recommend MegaSporeBiotic. It's the first broad-spectrum probiotic clinically shown to improve leaky gut by 60% in just 30 days. Megaspore biotic effectively reconditions the gut by increasing microbial diversity and encouraging the growth of key health promoting commensal gut bacteria.

  Bacillus strains have proven to be the most effective. MegaSpore contains 4 billion CFUs of 5 different strains of Bacillus that have been shocked back into their resilient spore form. No other spore-based probiotics have this feature.*This unique formula effectively reconditions the gut by increasing microbial diversity and encouraging the growth of key health-promoting, commensal gut bacteria. MegaSporeBiotic™

boasts a 5-year shelf-life, does not require refrigeration and maintains efficacy during antibiotic therapy.*

   * This statement has not been evaluated by the Food and Drug Administration. This product is not intended to diagnose, treat, cure, or prevent any disease.

- **Fish Oil :** Feed your brain, support your joints and promote cardiovascular health with pure EPA / DHA omega-3 fatty acids. I recommend EPA/DHA Marine Liquid from Premier Research Labs. It offers 1,000 mg. per serving of natural DHA and EPA from the original fish oil without molecular distillation. Their cold filtration process does not require high heat processing or the use of harsh solvents to separate the EPA and DHA. Finally a pure all natural fish oil! I also recommend Complete Hi-Potency Omega-3 Liquid from Nutri-Westand Omega Co3 from Apex Energetics.*

   * This statement has not been evaluated by the Food and Drug Administration. This product is not intended to diagnose, treat, cure, or prevent any disease.

What Do I Do If I Believe I Have Contracted the Coronavirus?

Don't panic, and check in with a call to your medical doctor. Proper testing will hopefully be available soon. It is best not to run to the doctor or hospital, for we need to keep these options available for the more vulnerable patients who get severe illness.

The Stages of coronavirus can have a few symptoms. The first is

1. Cough and fever, like any cold or flu.
2. The second stage occurs when the virus starts to move into the lungs. In this phase, patients will experience lung symptoms, like more coughing, phlegm, and possibly being short of breath.
3. In the third phase, the lungs become very inflamed, and it can be very hard to breath. Here is a CDC guideline for

symptoms: https://www.cdc.gov/coronavirus/2019-ncov/downloads/COVID19- symptoms.pdf Using natural medicine supplements can help with the first, second stages and is worth a shot in the third stage, especially if medical intervention is not available.

STAGE I: -

a. **Chicken soup** (See the recipe section), soups with garlic, ginger tea and warming chai spices: in this early phase of infection.

b. **Garlic** can be diced and added to anything: manuka honey and nut butter.

c. Fresh **ginger** made into foods and tea. (See the recipe section)

d. **Nasal Rinses**: (Neti pot)-Saline nasal irrigation is a therapy with roots in Ayurvedic medicine where you can bathe the nasal mucosa with a spray or liquid saline to help get rid of the mucus that is harboring the virus. Getting rid if it earlier may help prevent the virus from getting into the lungs.

e. **Elderberry** – A clinical trial of the flu showed that 15 1 tablespoon of elderberry four times a day for 5 days found significant relief and less time with the flu than a placebo and it's delicious.

f. **Zinc:** There is research suggesting that zinc in the early onset of a cold may help get rid of the cold. Taking zinc throughout the day, might be helpful. It is speculated that it can help deter the virus early on, before it gets into the lungs. I recommend taking 30 drops per day of **Eidon's ionic liquid zinc**. It's more easily absorbed than zinc tablets and is usually available.

g. Stay at home, don't have visitors. Shop online to receive packages and food - call for phone medical help if you need it - if you live with others, keep yourself in a ventilated bedroom (open windows), and don't share towels and toiletries - all waste should be double bagged.

FOR STAGE II and III, If the virus is moving into your lungs, besides contacting your physician, consider these options for **Advanced Immune Support:** I recommend Standard Process Andrographis Complex, Biocidin and Guna Flu for Advanced Immune Support.

- **Natural anti-viral herbs:** Many herbs have broad-spectrum antimicrobial effects or immune-enhancing effects. Formulas contain different immune boosters such as astragalus, green tea extract, andrographis, and monolaurin.

Stay at home, don't have visitors. Shop online to receive packages and food - call for phone medical help if you need it - if you live with others, keep yourself in a ventilated bedroom (open windows), and don't share towels and toiletries - all waste should be double bagged **FOR STAGE II and III**, If the Virus is moving into your lungs, besides contacting your physician, consider these options:

a. **Check your oxygen saturation with a pulse oximeter,** If you are feeling short of breath. Sometimes anxiety can feel like shortness of breath, and your oxygen levels are actually fine. Normal pulse oximeter readings usually range from 95 to 100 percent. Values under 90 percent are considered low. If yours is getting low, call your doctor right away. Here are some examples of pulse oximeters you can obtain: o https://amzn. to/2VSrMTH o https://amzn.to/2vBxpLr -

- **1. Andrographis Complex by Standard Process** contains a blend of herbs to support normal immune system function.

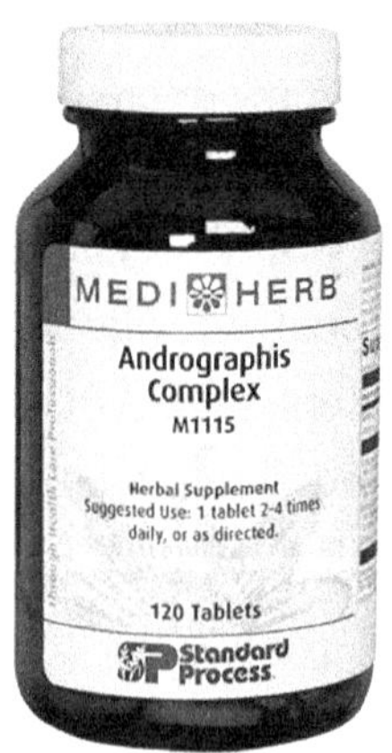

Andrographis is an ancient Chinese herb well known for sinus and respiratory support. It is often recommended for those with chronic sinus and lung congestion. Research shows it can work as a broad-spectrum antiviral to help restrain virus replication and virus-induced pathogenesis. Andrographis has already been shown, in cell tests, to be effective against avian influenza A (H9N2 and H5N1) and human influenza A H1N1 viruses, likely by stopping the ability of viruses to bind to our cells. Most specifically for coronavirus, it looks like it has the ability to help decrease expression of a protein called the ACE2 receptor that the Covid-19 latches on to in the lungs. This may be a key to prevent the big problems Covid-19 can cause. **Andrographis Complex** herbal formulation is used traditionally to:

- Help maintain healthy immune system function
- Support healthy immune system response
- Support healthy respiratory system function
- Support and maintain normal body temperature already in a normal range
- Encourage adaptive response to occasional everyday stress*

*This statement has not been evaluated by the Food and Drug Administration. This product is not intended to diagnose, treat, cure, or prevent any disease.

- **2. Biocidin® LSF** is a proprietary combination of botanicals directed at addressing microbial balance and the biofilms which often accompany pathogens and impede successful eradication. * This statement has not been evaluated by the Food and Drug Administration. This product is not intended to diagnose, treat, cure, or prevent any disease.

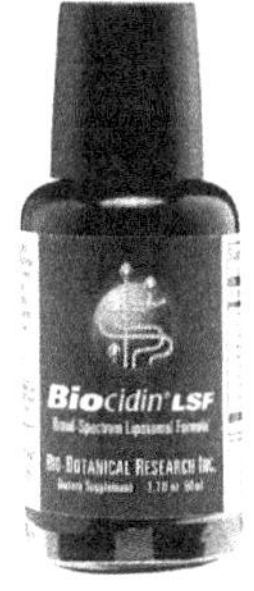

- **3. GUNA Flu** is an effective solution that contains ingredients to both help reduce the severity and duration of cold and flu symptoms. Guna-flu offers temporary relief of cold flu symptoms that may include: fever, headaches, or minor aches and pains. GUNA Flu is a homeopathic remedy from Guna biotherapeutics.* * This statement has not been evaluated by the Food and Drug Administration. This product is not intended to diagnose, treat, cure, or prevent any disease.

- 4. **Turmeric:**Turmeric has been shown to limit lung injury in pneumonia from influenza in lung cells by shutting down an inflammatory component of the immune system called Nf Kappa B. Turmeric supplements can help lower inflammation. In the patients who have severe and life-threatening illness, it is inflammation in the lungs that caused the most damage. I recommend **Turmero Active from Apex Energetics**.

- 5. **Vitamin C** take 1 gram of vitamin C every hour until you feel bowel discomfort. Count how many grams you took that day and repeat every day until well. Higher levels of vitamin C as used in intravenous therapy may help patients who have respiratory distress syndrome as well. If you are having lung issues, talk to your doctor about using www.InnerSourceHealth.com @InnerSourceH 14 intravenous vitamin C adjunctively to your conventional care. If you are in the hospital and breathing is severely compromised, ask your doctor about intravenous vitamin C therapy, which is being currently tested in South Korea, and has been shown in one case of ARDS to reverse a very severe syndrome. I recommend **Ecological Formulas Buffered Vitamin C Crystals** made from tapioca.

- 6. **Huang Lian Jie Du Tang** (HLJDT): The ancient Chinese herbal formula translated as "Coptis Decoction To Relieve Toxicity." In patients who have lung sickness from virus, it may help lower lung inflammation by lowering key factors involved in over-revving up the immune system which can cause damage in the lungs. While I recommend getting to a hospital for care if you can, it may be worth considering these herbs if a person has significant lung issues and cannot get proper hospital medical treatment for any reason. These herbs are meant to only be used for 1-2 weeks.

If you'd like to check out the immune support and other recommended supplements I've selected, here's a link to my online store:

advanced-weight-loss-wellness.square.site

I've set up the online store so you don't have to come in to pick up supplements. For your convenience, they
can be drop-shipped directly to your home.
 If you're not a current patient and would like to set up an appointment for a complimentary 15-minute nutritional consultation, or a chiropractic adjustment, you can contact me by phone at **925-962-9160**
or e-mail drrettner@sbcglobal.net**.**

FREE 15 MINUTE NUTRITIONAL CONSULTATION

go to drrettner.com and scroll down to the bottom of the page.

III. How chiropractic saved lives during the 1918 Flu Pandemic

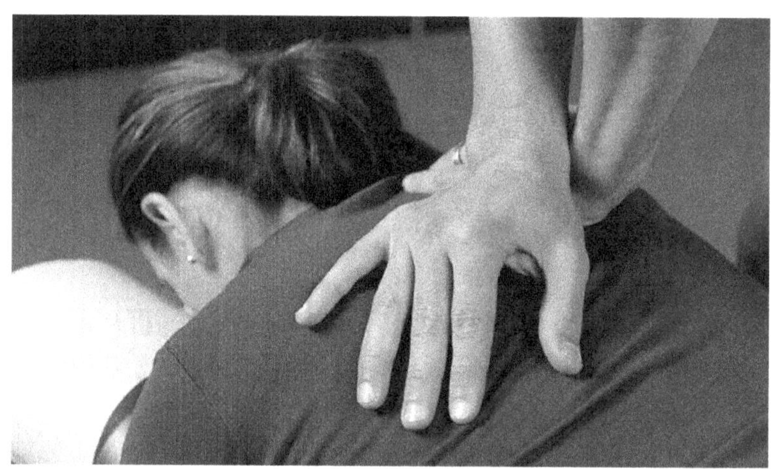

In the closing days of World War I, a deadly form of influenza appeared. The Spanish flu pandemic of 1917-1918 claimed more lives than the war. The 1918 Spanish flu infected 500 million people around the world and killed anywhere from 50 million to 100 million people, making it one of the deadliest epidemics in human history.

Very little was known about prevention or treatment of the flu virus back then and so the world was very much at the mercy of the deadly disease, at least so they thought. To better reference this time, Penicillin was discovered around 1926 and the first flu vaccine was used on soldiers in 1938.

Since science was still relatively in the dark ages in 1918, chiropractors relied on a philosophy of vitality, things natural, and adjusting for the removal of nerve interference as a rule. Application of these principles with the chiropractic adjustment as center piece, chiropractors witnessed a wide variety of health benefits including recovering from respiratory infections but the real test came during the Spanish Flu Pandemic of 1918.

Chiropractic is a profession that was really made by the 1918 flu. In 1918 chiropractic was brand-new. The first chiropractor adjusted the first patient in the year 1895. Chiropractic was just 23 years old when the flu struck. From 1917 to 1918 the people who had the flu who were dying and received chiropractic, their chances of survival increased dramatically. If they were already under chiropractic care, they tended to not come down with the flu. What independent health care observers noted was that those who chose chiropractic care had only one 40th the death rate as compared to those who chose allopathic or drug based management. This did not go unnoticed by public health authorities and the result was licensure for the chiropractic profession. Chiropractic was licensed in Iowa and Nebraska as a consequence of the observation that those under chiropractic care were not dying during the 1917-1918 flu epidemic in anywhere near the same proportion as compared to those who were under medical care.

During the aftermath, scientists and officials got busy investigating the forensics to learn more about what had just happened. To the surprise of the scientific community, the little-known chiropractic profession performed amazingly well around the country.

Some Interesting Statistics:

During the 1918 flu, researchers in Davenport, Iowa found that out of the 93,590 patients treated by medical doctors, there were 6,116 deaths — a loss of one patient out of every 15. Chiropractors at the Palmer School of Chiropractic adjusted 1,635 cases, with only one death. Outside Davenport, chiropractors in Iowa cared for 4,735 cases with only six deaths — one out of 866.

The medical profession was seeing a majority of the worst of the worst; however, one of the greatest statistics backing chiropractic care came from Oklahoma. During the same epidemic, in Oklahoma, out of 3,490 flu patients under chiropractic care, there were only seven deaths. Furthermore, chiropractors were called in to treat 233 cases given up as lost after medical treatment and reportedly saved all but 25 lives. In another report covering 4,193 cases by 213 chiropractors, 4,104 showed complete recovery.

Dr. M. L. Stanphill D.C. recounted meeting an elderly chiropractor in 1996 who told him that his introduction to chiropractic was doing house calls with his father, who was a chiropractor before him. He told him that those house calls were made specifically to treat people who were bedridden with infectious diseases, primarily pneumonia. He told him that his father had a reputation of having never lost a pneumonia patient. This was the pre-antibiotic era of health care. These results are part of the proven, critical link between the body's central nervous system and the immune system.1

Research:

A study by Ronald Pero, Ph.D., chief of cancer prevention research at New York's Preventive Medicine Institute and professor of medicine at New York University showed the positive effect that chiropractic care can have on the immune system and general health.

Dr. Pero measured the immune systems of people under chiropractic care as compared to those in the general population and those with cancer and other serious diseases. His initial three-year study was of 107 individuals who had been under chiropractic care for five years or more. The chiropractic patients were found to have a 200% greater immune competence than those people who had not received chiropractic care, and they had 400% greater immune competence than those people with cancer and other serious diseases. The immune system's superiority of those under chiropractic care did not appear to diminish with age. Dr. Pero stated: "When applied in a clinical framework, I have never seen a group other than this chiropractic group to experience a 200% increase over the normal patients. This is why it is so dramatically important. We have never seen such a positive improvement in a group."[2]

In 1994, Life Chiropractic University researchers took a group of HIV positive patients and adjusted them for six-months. They discovered that the "patients that were adjusted had a 48% increase in the number CD4 cells. CD4 cells are a critical part of immunity. The measurements were taken at the patients' independent medical center, where they were under medical supervision for the condition. The control group (patients that weren't adjusted) experienced the opposite effect with a 7.96% decrease in CD4 cell counts over the same period of time.[3]

The primary purpose for an adjustment is to remove any irritation or interference to the nerves, the information highway from the brain to the body.

When this information highway gets congested, the life force (innate intelligence) that runs through the nerves, telling the brain and body what is going on inside, cannot flow efficiently which results in a number of symptoms and diseases. Chiropractors allow the body to function as it was designed to do and, in turn, patient's struck with the flu were able to regain their health - without vaccines and drugs. An adjustment often stimulates the immune system to better fight off any challenge, including influenza.

Immune Benefits of the Chiropractic Adjustment:

1. Researchers have reported white blood cell (WBC) and immune boosting benefits of adjustments seen in blood tests. There is a barrage of white blood cell activity locally and those are the scavengers of bacteria and viruses. Viruses and bacteria are actively cleaned up by the WBCs thereby reducing illness.
2. There is also an effect on the peripheral end organ of the spinal nerve activated by the adjustment where the cells are more normally functioning with better blood flow and nerve flow to the organ and tissue.4

In regards to the flu, attention should be directed to the upper thoracic region, especially the upper rib articulations. Appropriate manipulation of the rib cage can help increase ventilation to the lungs.

During the 1918 Spanish flu pandemic, doctors of chiropractic noticed that their patients seemed to have a lower fatality rate than the general population. Although this chiropractic observation remains unpublished in the peer-reviewed literature (since no scholarly journals were willing to publish chiropractic data in those days). However, a study was published by the osteopathic profession. Among doctors of osteopathy of the time, it was routine to check patients' spines for "osteopathic lesions" (what chiropractors know as "subluxations"), and to correct them with manipulation. Due to this similarity, the osteopathic publication effectively verifies the chiropractic experience.

The death rate among influenza patients under conventional medical care in the U.S. was estimated at 5 percent to 6 percent. The fatality rate among influenza cases under osteopathic care was estimated at 0.25 percent. The implication drawn from this data by the study's author was that lesions (subluxations) depress the immune system; therefore, correcting the lesions assists immune function.5

It is so interesting to note from a historical perspective that chiropractors were licensed because of their ability to treat people with an infection, the flu. Reminding you that this was in the pre-antibiotic and the pre-vaccination era of healthcare. While today we mostly look at chiropractors as someone who treats sore backs and sore necks etc. Back in their history practically nobody went to chiropractors with aches and pains. They primarily went to chiropractors with infectious diseases. By way of having more flexibility and ease in the spine and spinal tissues, the nervous system is allowed to function at its most effective and optimal way. This relationship influences the way that our body can adapt to the environment and our immune systems can fight disease.

To maintain optimal health and energy, it's best to have a chiropractic adjustment once a week. If you're not a current patient and would like to set up an appointment for a chiropractic adjustment, you can contact me by phone at 925-962-9160 or e-mail drrettner@sbcglobal.net.

FREE 15 MINUTE NUTRITIONAL CONSULTATION

go to drrettner.com and scroll down to the bottom of the page.

IV. Sleep

During sleep, your immune system releases proteins called cytokines, some of which help promote sleep. In addition, infection-fighting antibodies and cells are reduced during periods when you don't get enough sleep. So, your body needs sleep to fight infectious diseases."The more all-nighters you pull, the more likely you are to decrease your body's ability to respond to viral infections." Researchers report sleep can help immune cells attach to targets and help fight infection. The study reveals how sleep assists the body in fighting infections, whereas conditions like chronic stress can make the body more susceptible to illness.

Although researchers aren't exactly sure how sleep boosts the immune system, it's clear that getting enough - usually 7 to 9 hours for an adult - is key for good health. I've had sleep issues my whole life so I've done a lot of research on solutions. If you'd like some help getting a better night's sleep, I wrote an e-book "10 Secrets to a Good Nights Sleep and That Your Doctor Won't Tell You."

If you'd like some help getting a better night's sleep, I wrote an e-book "10 Secrets to a Good Night's Sleep That Your Doctor Won't Tell You." If you'd like a copy please go to www.chirovideo.com

FREE 15 MINUTE NUTRITIONAL CONSULTATION

go to drrettner.com and scroll down to the bottom of the page.

V. Exercise

Try to get regular, moderate exercise, like a daily 30-minute walk, hiking, gardening or cycling. I personally hike or bike at least 40 minutes per day, 7 days a week. Adults should be physically active in some way every day, and do at least 150 minutes a week of moderate aerobic activity. It can help your immune system fight off an infection.

Exercise can also boost serotonin, your body's feel-good chemical and help you sleep better. Both of those are good for your immune system.

For a breathing exercise that may help support a healthy immune system, watch the YouTube video "Wim Hof breathing tutorial by Wim Hof".

VI. Sauna

A recent Chinese investigation suggests COVID-19 is highly sensitive to temperatures and spreads faster in colder climates; its most rapid spread is occurring at a temperature of 47.7°F.

Our body fights off viruses by raising core body temperature. Fever is a mechanism by which your body fights viral infection. We can simulate a fever by raising your core body temperature in a sauna, steam bath or by engaging in physical exercise to induce sweating.

A number of studies have investigated the anti-viral effects of sauna bathing. For example, a clinical study involving 50 volunteers showed regular sauna bathers and half the rate of common cold compared to non-users. Those who use a sauna at least 2 or 3 times per week also had a lower risk of influenza and pneumonia.

Sauna use kills bacteria, fungi, parasites and viruses and boost your immune function by increasing white blood cell, lymphocyte, neutrophil and basophil counts. By elevating your core temperature your body also releases heat shock proteins that help block the replication of influenza viruses. Thus, sauna therapy may have potential against RNA viruses particularly prior or early on in infection.

Coronaviruses (as a general group) incubate in your sinuses for about three days before moving down into your lungs and appear to be destroyed by temperatures around 133°F which can easily be really reached in a sauna.

German research showed that animals placed in a sauna before being injected with influenza virus had dramatically reduced lung pathology and mortality. Viral replication was also suppressed in sauna-exposed animals.

Sauna bathing has also been shown to improve respiratory function in those with asthma, bronchitis and obstructive pulmonary disease and can boost your mood — an added boon if you're struggling with stress and anxiety.

Sauna bathing is one way to help render viruses inactive prior to entering the body. It has been studied that high temperatures and especially moist heat with water vapor can deactivate viruses effectively. Even at a temperature of 55-70 ° C (moist heat), the virus can be countered within a few minutes and thus there is a loss of infectivity (Böhm, R. 2002. Virusinaktivierung). Sauna itself is not a cure to infections but it can help reduce the chances of catching a flu and other illnesses. Part of the sauna bathing routine includes washing before and after the sauna, helping to prevent transmission via physical contact.

Already sick and you don't have access to a sauna... Make an herbal facial sauna: Add 2 cups of water to a large pot that measures about 5 inches high by 10 inches wide. Bring the water to a boil then turn it off. Add 5-10 drops of oregano essential oil or eucalyptus essential oil. Make a "tent" of a large bath towel over your head and over the pot. The towel helps keep the scent of the oils and steam near your face instead of just escaping into the air. As you lean over the pot, inhale the fumes from the essential oil. Don't get too close to the steam or the pot or you could risk getting a nasty steam burn! You want to be close enough that it feels comfortably hot, like a sauna, but not too close. Use only filtered water.

VII. Recipes to Support a Healthy Immune System

Bone Broth

Ingredients:
- 1 gallon of water
- 2 tbsp apple cider vinegar
- 2–4 pounds of animal bones
- Sea Salt to taste

Directions:
1. Place all ingredients in a large pot or slow cooker.
2. Bring to a boil.
3. Reduce to a simmer and cook for 12–24 hours. The longer it cooks, the better it will taste and more nutritious it will be.
4. Allow the broth to cool. Strain it into a large container and discard the solids.

In order to make the most nutritious broth, it is best to use a variety of bones — marrow bones, oxtail, knuckles and feet. You can even mix and match bones in the same batch.

Adding vinegar is important because it helps pull all of the valuable nutrients out of the bones and into the water, which is ultimately what you will be consuming.

You can also add vegetables, herbs or spices to your broth to enhance the flavor.

Common additions include garlic, onion, celery, carrot, parsley and thyme. These can be added right away in step one.

Where to Get Bones

Instead of throwing leftover bones and carcasses from meals in the garbage, save them to make broth.

You can collect the bones in a bag and store them in your freezer until you are ready to cook them.

However, if you are not someone who typically buys and eats whole chickens and bone-in meat, you may wonder where you can find animal bones to make broth.

You can ask for them at your local butcher or farmers market. The meat department at most grocery stores will often have them too.

The best part is they are very inexpensive to purchase. Your butcher may even give them to you for free.

Do your best to find pastured chicken or grass-fed beef bones, since these animals will be the healthiest and provide maximum health benefits to you.

How to Store It

While it's easiest to make broth in large batches, it can only be stored safely in the refrigerator for up to five days.

To help your broth last longer, you can freeze it in small containers and heat up individual servings as needed.

Immune-Boosting Soup

Whenever I feel a bit "under the weather," this is my go-to soup recipe.

Ingredients

- 3 tbsp expeller pressed coconut oil
- 1 large onion, chopped
- 2 cups carrots, chopped
- 2 cups celery , chopped
- 3 cups kabocha or other winter squash, peeled, seeded and cubed
- 1 T garlic, peeled and minced
- 1-2 tbsp ginger root, peeled and minced
- 2 cups cabbage, sliced thinly and chopped
- 8 shiitake mushrooms, sliced
- 8 cups chicken or vegetable stock, preferably homemade
- 2 cups shredded roasted chicken or turkey (optional)
- 1 tsp sea salt, or more to taste
- 1 tsp dried turmeric or 1 tbsp fresh grated turmeric root
- 2 sheets of nori, cut into thin strips
- 1 cup fresh cilantro leaves, chopped

Directions:

- In a large pot, melt coconut oil over medium heat and sauté the onions until softened. Add the garlic and ginger and stir for another minute or so. Add the carrots, celery and squash, and cook about 5-10 minutes, stirring occasionally.
- Add remaining ingredients to the pot, except for cilantro and nori. Cover and bring to a boil.
- Reduce the heat to low and simmer for about 20 minutes, until vegetables are tender. Stir in the nori strips and adjust seasonings to taste.
- Top each bowl with a handful of cilantro and enjoy.

Variation: To make this a lovely Miso Vegetable soup, omit the chicken, and just before serving, stir a tablespoon of miso paste into some hot broth in the serving bowl. Ladle in the rest of the soup and stir well before serving. Be sure not to cook the miso paste.

Marcelle's chicken soup

Serves 4 to 6

This is one of my mothers most sought after recipes. Friday night would not be the same without it. Chicken soup is known to give a boost to the immune system.

Ingredients:

- 2 chicken wings, one neck and the bottom half of a 4 pound chicken
- 1 large onion quartered
- 2 carrots diced
- 1 parsnip quartered
- 2 celery stalks and leaves, cut into large slices
- 1 teaspoon sea salt to taste
- 3-4 cloves of garlic
- 2 tsp. Herbs de Provence
- 1 sprig of parsley per bowl

Place in a large pot with 3 1/2 quarts of water. Bring to a boil and remove any fat that rises to the top. Add the remaining ingredients except for the parsley. Turn to a simmer and keep covered for 2 1/2 hours on a very low heat. Add water as needed. Strain off the bones. When serving, place one sprig of parsley in each bowl.

MAITAKE SOUP

Maitake boost your immune system by strengthening the natural killer cells.

Ingredients:
- 1 package Maitake mushroom
- 2 tsp. garlic
- 4 tsp. ginger
- 1 long green onion
- 1 cups chicken broth
- 1 T soy sauce
- 1 tsp. olive oil
- 1 tsp. sesame oil

Turmeric Tea

Ingredients:
- 5 cups water
- 2 inches of turmeric root, thinly sliced, or grated with skin on
- 1 to 2 inches of ginger root, thinly sliced or grated
- ½ tsp. cinnamon
- 1 organic lemon, peeled and then juiced, try not to peel the white part.
- Few cracks of pepper
- 1 tsp. coconut oil
- 1 tsp. honey, to taste

Directions:

Pour the 5 cups of water into a saucepan and heat over medium heat until it just comes to a boil. Add the turmeric, ginger, pepper, cinnamon, and lemon peel and simmer for 10 minutes. Do not boil.

Pour the tea through a fine strainer into a large bowl or large measuring cup. Add the juice from 1 lemon and stir. At this point you can pour a cup of tea and add 1 tsp. Coconut oil and 1 tsp. of honey, stir and enjoy. The rest of the tea can be stored in a mason jar in the refrigerator for up to 3 days. Each time you heat up some tea, just add some coconut oil and honey for your serving, having all the wonderful medicinal benefits.

Celery Juice

Drink 16 or more ounces of plain, freshly made celery juice every morning on an empty stomach.

Ingredients: one large bunch of celery directions rinse the celery and run it through a juicer. Drink immediately for best results.

Cucumber Juice

Cucumber juice has a cooling effect on organs which makes it a wonderful fever reducer. Sip on plain, freshly made cucumber juice from 1-2 organic cucumbers whenever you have a fever. Drink immediately for best results.

Fresh Ginger Tea

To create this tea, follow these steps:

- Juice one to two pounds of ginger, and place juice in a jar and refrigerate.
- Place two to four ounces of ginger juice in a mug with the juice of one-half lemon and a large tablespoon of honey.
- Add one-eighth teaspoon of cayenne pepper and six ounces of hot water.

Drink two to six cups of this per day, sipping slowly throughout the day.

Ginger Water

Ginger is a powerful anti-viral one of gingers special qualities is it ability to bring the body out of a reactive state which can happen easily when a virus or bug is on the scene set this ginger water throughout the day.

Ingredients:

- 1 to 2 inches of fresh ginger
- 2 cups water
- half lemon (optional)
- 2 teaspoons or a honey (optional)

Grate the ginger into 2 cups of water and add the juice of half a lemon. Allow the water to steep for at least 15 minutes and ideally longer. You can even leave it steeping in the fridge overnight. Strain the water. Add lemon and raw honey, if desired and enjoy warm or cold throughout the day.

Tips: As an alternative to grating the ginger, try chopping it into into a few small pieces and squeeze them in a garlic press-it will act like a mini juicer. Be sure to take out the pulp from the press afterwards, Chop it finely and add it to the water, as well.

2 Chinese Herb Tea Recipes for Immune-Boosting:

1. Stephen Harrod Buhner's Botanical Formula

For this formula, you'll need to combine:
- Three parts *Cordyceps*
- Two parts *Angelica sinensis*
- One part *Rhodiola*
- One part *Astragalus*

Take one teaspoon of this formula three times per day for protection against infection. Take one teaspoon six times per day if you're experiencing symptoms.

2. Shuang-Huang-Lian Antiviral Formula

For this formula, you'll need to combine:
- Two parts *Forsythia suspensa* (also known as lian qiao or weeping forsythia plant)
- One part *Lonicera japonica* (also called jin yin hua or Japanese honeysuckle)
- One part *Scutellaria baicalensis* (also known as huang qin or Chinese skullcap)

Take one teaspoon of this formula three times per day. It's best to take it in combination with immune-boosting herb the sick who are most at risk.

VIII. Essential Oils & Colloidal Silver

Covid-19 Prevention and Treatment: A Chinese Medicine Doctor's Guide by Noach Bittelman, L.Ac.

Anyone with a strong pre-existing condition, including pregnancy, is recommended to consult with a qualified professional before beginning any of the following recommendations.

Prevention Strategies for Covid-19

1. Oregano Oil

Oregano oil is a very strong antibacterial and antiviral substance. Oregano oil should be purchased already diluted in olive oil, not the straight essential oil. The P73 Oreganol strain is a very strong formulation of wild oregano, but the regular oregano oil should work just fine. It is important to get the oregano oil in a liquid solution, not in a capsule, pill, or tablet. This is because we want the oregano oil vapors to get to the lungs, which as noted above is one of the two primary areas COVID-19 attacks. Using it in pill form will be less effective for the lungs, although it will work very well for the digestive tract. Make sure you can strongly smell the oregano when you open the bottle of oregano oil, as you don't want to use something that is a cheaply produced weak substance.

Oregano oil is the first choice in our attempt to prevent or mitigate COVID-19 because it treats the two systems that this coronavirus primarily attacks, the Lungs/respiratory and Spleen/digestive systems.

In order to maximize the effectiveness of the oregano oil you must administer it correctly. Place 3-5 drops on the middle of the tongue and hold it there without swallowing. As the vapors from the oil start to release, breathe in deeply through your mouth and hold the breath in your lungs around 5 seconds, then slowly breathe out through your nose. Repeat this process 10 times, then slowly swallow the oil. This will maximize the oil getting to your lungs on the inhalation and passing through your sinuses on the exhalation.

Repeat the oregano oil treatment twice a day. If you are in a relatively low-risk situation you can reduce the oregano oil to once per day, adding an extra dose if you feel you may have been potentially exposed to the virus. If you are in a high-risk environment, or exposed to those who have COVID-19, you can also dab a drop or two of the oregano oil just below your nose on the "mustache" area, or put a drop on your hands and bring the hands up to your nose to inhale the vapors a few times an hour. No, it doesn't taste good, and it may burn a bit as you swallow it, but you'll get used to it. If it's absolutely unworkable undiluted you can try putting it in a small amount of water and then following the above instructions. The oregano oil treatment can be administered anytime, although 30-60 minutes after eating will be easier for those who have sensitive stomachs.

Digestive disturbances including diarrhea is being reported more prominently from various locales around the world. Oregano oil, as mentioned above, effects primarily the respiratory and digestive systems, something which confirms it as a top choice for preventing and treating this illness.

Diffusing Essential Oils:

The diffusing of essential oils in your home or work environment can help you prevent infection. It's not so much that the essential oils will kill the virus in the environment, although that may in fact also happen, it's more that you will be breathing the essential oils as they are dispersed in the atmosphere and they will then exert their effect on your body from the inside. Remember, COVID-19 has a very strong affinity for the lungs, so diffused essential oils with antiviral properties which are breathed in are a very appropriate delivery route to deal with this virus.

The question is which essential oils to use. Based on researched use of essential oils for their antiviral properties, especially in regards to coronavirus, a combination of Eucalyptus, Ravensara Aromatica, Tea Tree, and Bay Laurel (Laurus Nobilis) should work well to help prevent or mitigate against COVID-19 infection.

Place two drops of each of the above oils in a diffuser device and diffuse into your environment twice per day. It is easy to rig up a diffusing set up, so there is no need to buy a special diffuser. Simply put some water in a bowl, add the essential oils, and set up a lit candle under the bowl. The heat from the candle will warm the water and the essential oils and they will start to vaporize and diffuse. No need to stand near the bowl and breathe in the vapors, just go about your business and breathe regularly as the vapors fill the atmosphere of the room. If you are treating a large space you may need to set up two or more diffusers in different parts of the space.

If you are unable to set up a diffuser device, you can apply a drop of the oils to the palm of one hand and rapidly rub your palms together until the oil becomes vaporized from the heat, about 15 seconds. Then bring your hands, cupped together but partly open, up to your face and breathe in deeply a few times, holding in the breath for 5-10 seconds. As the strength of the vapors wanes rub the hands together again and repeat the process, 5-10 repetitions are sufficient. It is best to close your eyes as you breathe in since the essential oil vapors are very strong; likewise it is best to avoid touching any mucous membranes directly with the oils.

If you can only get three of the above oils, use three. If you can only get two or even just one oil, use what you can get. Remember, a little bit of help could be just enough to help your body's immune system overcome the virus.

2. Colloidal Silver

Colloidal Silver is such a fantastic antibacterial and antiviral substance that it should perhaps be at the top of the list. It's extremely useful for many bacterial and viral conditions. I have used it with many patients over the years with great success both internally and topically, treating dangerous infections such as MRSA, pneumonia, and sepsis conditions. It is an excellent antiviral and antibacterial, and should be in everyone's medicine cabinet. If someone were to become ill with COVID-19 colloidal silver would be a strong choice as part of a treatment strategy. However, it would be contraindicated in the cold and damp stage of the infection, when the tongue has thick white coating.

<u>Basic COVID-19 Treatment Protocol for Essential Oils:</u>

The following recommendations should be used <u>together</u> for best effect.

The four essential oils listed in the Prevention section of this paper: Eucalyptus, Ravensera Aromatica, Bay Leaf (Laurus Nobilis), and Tea Tree, should likewise be used as a treatment strategy, and as is true of the other recommended substances, the intensity of the treatment should be increased. The oils should be vaporized in the close vicinity of the patient on an ongoing basis, day and night.

1. Oregano Oil

P73 Oreganol is the desired strain; if it is unavailable use whatever oregano oil, diluted in olive oil, is available. The oregano oil should have a very strong, pungent aroma when you open the bottle; if this is not the case it is an indication of an inferior product and a different brand should be purchased if possible. As with the prevention strategy, the liquid form is more desirable than pill form. Encourage the patient to use the inhalation strategy outlined above in the prevention component of this paper, but if they are too weak to do strong inhalations simply have them hold the oil on their tongue and swallow slowly.

If there are concurrent digestive symptoms add in oregano oil in pill/capsule form. Again, the P73 Oreganol strain is the desired medicine, but if it is unavailable use whatever you can get.

Dosage:

Oil: 5 drops on the tongue, every 3-4 hours.

Pills/Capsules: 1 pill every 3-4 hours

The oil and pills can be used together when there are both respiratory and digestive symptoms. I have used Oregano oil clinically over the years with great success to treat both viral and bacterial infections; the oil has been shown in both in vitro and in vivo research to have antiviral and antibacterial effects, including against the coronavirus responsible for the SARS epidemic of 2003-2004.[ii][iii][iv]

COVID-19 Treatment Protocol Colloidal/Ionic Silver:

The dosage of colloidal or ionic silver varies depending on the manufacturer. In critical situations it is better to err by giving a higher dose of colloidal silver rather than a lower dose. Some manufacturers will list a "maintenance dose" and a "treatment dose". Use the recommended treatment dose. If it is homemade colloidal silver use ½-1 teaspoon per dose. The colloidal silver should be given every 2 hours in critical situations, and every 3-4 hours in serious situations.

If a nebulizer is available the colloidal silver liquid can be put into the nebulizer and inhaled directly into the lungs. This is the first choice delivery system; if there is no nebulizer simply have the patient swallow the silver.

As mentioned above, I have used Colloidal Silver successfully in the treatment of numerous acute conditions over the years, and in spite of continuous attempts to discredit colloidal silver, the research and clinical experience of medical personnel around the world continues to accumulate.

IX. Pandemic Humor

Stress relief from laughter? It's no joke

When it comes to relieving stress, more giggles and guffaws are just what the doctor ordered. Here's why:

By Mayo Clinic Staff

Whether you're guffawing at a sitcom on TV or quietly giggling at a newspaper cartoon, laughing does you good. Laughter is a great form of stress relief, and that's no joke.

Stress relief from laughter

A good sense of humor can't cure all ailments, but data is mounting about the positive things laughter can do.

Short-term benefits:

A good laugh has great short-term effects. When you start to laugh, it doesn't just lighten your load mentally, it actually induces physical changes in your body. Laughter can:

- **Stimulate many organs.** Laughter enhances your intake of oxygen-rich air, stimulates your heart, lungs and muscles, and increases the endorphins that are released by your brain.
- **Activate and relieve your stress response.** A rollicking laugh fires up and then cools down your stress response, and it can increase and then decrease your heart rate and blood pressure. The result? A good, relaxed feeling.
- **Soothe tension.** Laughter can also stimulate circulation and aid muscle relaxation, both of which can help reduce some of the physical symptoms of stress.

Long-term effects:

Laughter isn't just a quick pick-me-up, though. It's also good for you over the long term. Laughter may:

- **Improve your immune system.** Negative thoughts manifest into chemical reactions that can affect your body by bringing more stress into your system and decreasing your immunity. By contrast, positive thoughts can actually release neuropeptides that help fight stress and potentially more-serious illnesses.
- **Relieve pain.** Laughter may ease pain by causing the body to produce its own natural painkillers.
- **Increase personal satisfaction.** Laughter can also make it easier to cope with difficult situations. It also helps you connect with other people.
- **Improve your mood.** Many people experience depression, sometimes due to chronic illnesses. Laughter can help lessen your depression and anxiety and may make you feel happier.

Since laughter is so good for your immune system take a dose of the following:

Half of us are going to come out of this quarantine as amazing cooks. The other half will come out with a drinking problem.
****

Still haven't decided where to go for Easter ----- The Living Room or The Bedroom.
****

Homeschooling is going well. 2 students suspended for fighting and 1 teacher fired for drinking on the job. **********
I don't think anyone expected that when we changed the clocks we'd go from Standard Time to the Twilight Zone.
****

Quarantine Day 5: Went to this restaurant called THE KITCHEN. You have to gather all the ingredients and make your own meal. I have no clue how this place is still in business.
****

Day 6 of Homeschooling: My child just said "I hope I don't have the same teacher next year".... I'm offended.
****

My body has absorbed so much soap and disinfectant lately that when I pee it cleans the toilet.
****

I'm so excited --- it's time to take out the garbage. What should I wear?
****

Classified Ad: Single man with toilet paper seeks woman with hand sanitizer for good clean fun.
****

It's important to wear your mask at home, so you don't eat so much
****

X. The Real Pandemic Is Insulin Resistance

After old age, obesity appears to be the most prominent risk factor for being hospitalized with COVID-19, doubling the risk of hospitalization and patients under the age of 60. "Obesity may be one of the most important predictors of severe coronavirus illness, new studies say. It's an alarming finding for the United States, which has one of the highest obesity rates in the world."According to The New York Times,17 one hypothesis for why obesity is worsening COVID-19 has to do with the fact that obesity causes chronic inflammation. Obesity also makes you more vulnerable to infectious diseases by lowering your immune function.18,19,20,21,22,23

The real pandemic appears to be insulin resistance. When your body is insulin resistant,25 the cells in your body do not respond well to insulin, which lowers their ability to use glucose from the blood for energy. The pancreas secretes more insulin, trying to overcome the cells' weak response in their attempt to keep blood glucose levels in a healthy range.

Insulin resistance, in turn, is a diet-induced condition. Specifically, processed foods — which are loaded with added sugars, processed grains and industrially processed omega-6 vegetable oils. These include: Corn oil, safflower oil, sesame oil, soybean oil, sunflower oil, and walnut oil. They are the primary culprits causing insulin resistance, Type 2 diabetes and obesity.

Cytokine Storm-Why people die from COVID-19
Higher blood glucose levels appear to play a significant role in viral replication and the development of cytokine storms. Cytokines are released by your immune system in response to foreign invaders. In some cases, this immune response goes into overdrive, resulting in what's known as a "cytokine storm" that can cause severe tissue damage and lead to death. A cytokine storm response is typically the reason why people die from COVID-19.

What and When to Eat to Beat Insulin Resistance
Intermittent fasting promotes insulin sensitivity and improves blood sugar.27 This is important not only for helping both Type 2 diabetes and obesity.

Time restricted eating, mimics the eating habits of our ancestors and restores your body to a more natural state that allows a whole host of metabolic benefits to occur. Consider skipping breakfast and having your lunch at 11 a.m. and dinner at 6 p.m., making sure you stop eating three hours before bed. It's a great way to get results without a making other dietary changes.

One of the best ways to become more insulin sensitive and lose weight is by adopting a cyclical ketogenic diet, which involves limiting carbs and replacing them with healthy fats and moderate amounts of protein until you're at your ideal weight, ultimately allowing your body to burn fat — not carbohydrates — as its primary fuel.Once you reach this state, as evidenced by your ability to generate ketones over 5 mmol/l in your blood, then it is important to reintroduce healthy carbs back into your diet. Sweet potatoes would be a great example. If you fail to do this, the health of your microbiome will likely suffer.

Key Steps to Getting — and Staying — Healthy:
Avoid all processed sugar, instead use Stevia and Monk fruit. Monk fruit is granular and sweet with no calories and zero on the glycemic index.
Limit net carbs (total carbohydrates minus fiber) and protein and replace them with higher amounts of high-quality healthy fats such as nuts, seeds, olives, olive oil, avocados, coconut oil and grass fed free range meat.
Avoid all processed foods, including processed meats.
Avoid omega-6 vegetable oils: Corn oil, safflower oil, sesame oil, soybean oil, sunflower oil, and walnut oil.
Get regular exercise every day and increase physical movement throughout waking hours, with the goal of sitting down less than three hours a day.
Get sufficient sleep- Most people need around eight hours per night. Research has shown that sleep deprivation can significantly affect insulin sensitivity and immune function.

Stress management should be a regular part of your immune support. If you're chronically stressed or anxious, release the stress with chiropractic adjustments and the Chakra Armor Release of Emotions (CARE) technique on a regular basis. You'll walk in stressed out and walk out blissed out.

Optimize your gut health by regularly eating fermented foods such as sauerkraut, kimchi, Kevita and dairy free yogurt. It's also helpful to take high-quality probiotic supplements.

Optimize your vitamin D level Ideally through sensible sun exposure. If using D3 supplement make sure to take magnesium and vitamin K2 as well, as these nutrients work together.

Conclusion:

Robust immune function is necessary to effectively combat COVID-19. Health care really needs to start emphasizing strategies known to improve overall health rather than throwing drugs at symptoms that don't address the underlying causes.

If we want people to survive the next pandemic, then improving public health has got to be the No. 1 priority going forward. Waiting for a drug cure or vaccine is a fool's game.

If you're struggling to lose weight and you're not a current patient and would like to find out how you can be helped, I suggest setting up an appointment for a complimentary 15-minute weight loss consultation. You can contact me by phone at 925-962-9160 or by e-mail drrettner@sbcglobal.net

FREE 15 MINUTE NUTRITIONAL CONSULTATION

go to drrettner.com and scroll down to the bottom of the page.

The advanced weight loss and wellness program consists of:
 * Nutritional Consultations
 * Food Allergy Testing
 * Hormone Testing
 * Weight Loss Supplements and Shakes
 * Customized Detox Cleanse
 * Diet Diary and Weekly Check-in's
 * Chiropractic and
 * emotional support. It also includes Lipo Light and Whole Body Vibration sessions where you can lose between a 1/2 inch and 3 inches in 20 minutes.

Addendum: Preventive Health Practices

1. Wash your hands frequently

Regularly and thoroughly clean your hands with an alcohol-based hand rub or wash them with soap and water.

Why? Washing your hands with soap and water or using alcohol-based hand rub kills viruses that may be on your hands.

2. Maintain social distancing

Maintain at least 6 feet distance between yourself and anyone who is coughing or sneezing.

Why? When someone coughs or sneezes they spray small liquid droplets from their nose or mouth which may contain virus. If you are too close, you can breathe in the droplets, including the COVID-19 virus if the person coughing has the disease.

3. Avoid touching eyes, nose and mouth

Why? Hands touch many surfaces and can pick up viruses. Once contaminated, hands can transfer the virus to your eyes, nose or mouth. From there, the virus can enter your body and can make you sick.

4. Practice respiratory hygiene

Make sure you, and the people around you, follow good respiratory hygiene. This means covering your mouth and nose with your bent elbow or tissue when you cough or sneeze. Then dispose of the used tissue immediately.

Why? Droplets spread virus. By following good respiratory hygiene you protect the people around you from viruses such as cold, flu and COVID-19.

5. If you have fever, cough and difficulty breathing, seek medical care early

Stay home if you feel unwell. If you have a fever, cough and difficulty breathing, seek medical attention and call in advance. Follow the directions of your local health authority.

Why? National and local authorities will have the most up to date information on the situation in your area. Calling in advance will allow your health care provider to quickly direct you to the right health facility. This will also protect you and help prevent spread of viruses and other infections.

6. **Sneeze or cough into a tissue, then throw it out:** this is probably the best way to stop the spread of virus to others, if you have it. Don't sneeze into your hands, for then you can spread the virus even better with your hands onto surfaces. If you don't have a tissue, sneeze into your elbow, and then wash that clothing when possible, for virus can hang on there for days if not washed.

7. **Recipe for homemade hand sanitizer virus-fighter:**
- 2/3 cup of 91% alcohol

- 1/4 cup aloe vera gel

- Optional: a few drops of your favorite calming essential oil (like lavender) mix and place in container

Recommended YouTube videos for prevention:

1. How to Safely Grocery Shop During Coronavirus
https://youtu.be/TKx-F4AKteE

2. Grocery Shopping Tips in COVID-19 Revised (March 31, 2020)
Thorough Hand-Washing
https://www.youtube.com/channel/UCF9IOB2TExg3QIBupFtBDxg

3. Wim Hof breathing tutorial by Wim Hof
https://youtu.be/nzCaZQqAs9I

Conclusion

If we all stay calm, avoid the pandemic of fear, follow our common sense, and take care of ourselves and our families we can weather this and dramatically reduce sickness and death. But we have to come together (at least 6 feet apart!) as humans, and as a society to combat this pandemic. I hope this finds you safe and well. During this challenging time most of us are looking for ways to maintain optimal health and prevent getting sick from the Corona virus. You can wait for a year or more for a vaccine to be developed or try to make your immune system stronger now.

I have consulted with a licensed clinical nutritionist and a functional medicine doctor to put together a research-based supplement protocol designed to strengthen your immune system and another supplement protocol if you should become sick. These supplements are professional-grade nutraceuticals and are in very high demand at this time. It's best not to wait because they may be out of stock in the future when you need them the most. Because of the pandemic, zinc and Vitamin C often take months to obtain. Fortunately I have found high-quality sources for both that are available at this time.

If you'd like to check out the immune support and other recommended supplements I've selected, here's a link to my online store: advanced-weight-loss-wellness.square.site

I've set up the online store so you don't have to come in to pick up supplements. For your convenience, they can be drop-shipped directly to your home.

If you're not a current patient and would like to set up an appointment for a complimentary 15-minute nutritional consultation, or a chiropractic adjustment, you can contact me by phone at 925-962-9160 or e-mail drrettner@sbcglobal.net

FREE 15 MINUTE NUTRITIONAL CONSULTATION
go to drrettner.com and scroll down to the bottom of the page.

* Note: This e-book is not intended to provide medical advice and any changes should be done in consultation with your healthcare provider.

Sources and References:

1. The Official History Of Chiropractic in Texas By Walter R Rhodes, DC Published by the Texas Chiropractic Association 1978

2. Pero R. "Medical Researcher Excited By CBSRF Project Results." The Chiropractic Journal, August 1989; 32.

3. "The Effects of Specific Upper Cervical Adjustments on the CD4 Counts of HIV Positive Patients." The Chiro Research Journal; 3(1); 1994

4. Super Viruses; the 1918 flu Pandemic and Chiropractic Laura Sheehan (The adjustment has 2 benefits)

5. Riley GW. Osteopathic success in the treatment of influenza and pneumonia. J Am Osteopathic Assn, 1919; 18:565

6. The Real Pandemic Is Insulin Resistance Analysis by Dr. Joseph Mercola May 4, 2020

7. New York Times April 16, 2020 (Archived)

8. Obesityaction.org Obesity and the Immune System

9. J Am. Diet Assoc. 1999; 99(3): 294-299

10. Obesity Reviews 2001; 2: 131-140 (PDF)

11. Journal of Obesity 2013, Article ID 616193

12. JCI January 3, 2017

13. Advances in Nutrition January 7, 2016; 7(1): 66-75

14. Proc Nutr Soc 2012 May;71(2):298-306

15. Science November 16, 2018; 362(6416): 770-775